YOUR KNOWLEDGE HAS VALUE

Bibliographic information published by the German National Library:

The German National Library lists this publication in the National Bibliography; detailed bibliographic data are available on the Internet at http://dnb.dnb.de .

Imprint:

Copyright © 2016 GRIN Verlag
Print and binding: Books on Demand GmbH, Norderstedt Germany
ISBN: 9783346200945

This book at GRIN:

https://www.grin.com/document/591448

Kamrul Islam

Personal Development Portfolio. Theory and Personal Objectives

GRIN Verlag

GRIN - Your knowledge has value

Since its foundation in 1998, GRIN has specialized in publishing academic texts by students, college teachers and other academics as e-book and printed book. The website www.grin.com is an ideal platform for presenting term papers, final papers, scientific essays, dissertations and specialist books.

Visit us on the internet:

http://www.grin.com/

http://www.facebook.com/grincom

http://www.twitter.com/grin_com

PERSONAL DEVELOPMENT PORTFOLIO

Leadership For Professional Development

Kamrul Islam

Semester: August 2016

Table of Contents

1. Introduction

Over the last decade personal development plan (PDP) has been topical for many reasons particularly to create an action plan for future. The personal development plan is also known as personal enterprise plan (PEP) and individual development plan (IDP) normally incorporates a statement of one's education, competencies or strengths & weaknesses, aspirations, training, and steps to illustrate how the plan is to be ascertained. There is no single perfect definition to demonstrate personal development plan. Different author has interpreted PDP in different characteristics or habitual manner.

Ellwood (2011) defined PDP as the process of generating an action plan based on reflection, awareness, objective setting and making synopsis for personal development in the substance of self-improvement, education or for career where Kotter, 1995 interpreted PDP as a tool that assists an individual to learn from experience and accelerate to accomplish the required outcomes and objectives.

Nevertheless, Rouse, 2005 in his article *"Personal development"* concluded Personal development plan as a statement of an individual's lifestyle and career priorities, career positioning, exploration of opportunities, identifying risks and generate an alternative plan to achieve desired goals and objectives. Therefore, PDP is the process which is outlined to enable an individual to reflect and construct a planning for academic, personal, and career development of an individual. By engaging with PDP an individual will be benefited in following ways.

- *Enhance self- awareness of an individual- who he/her is and what the individual want.*

- *Determine the skill and expertise that an individual has already gained and identify the gaps that they need to achieve.*

- *Originate adequate appropriate plan to obtain the expertise and skills that an individual requires for academic studies and desired career path.*

The aims and objective of this personal development portfolio identify and analyse my current situation with the utilisation of SWOT analysis and to reflect on my previous learning by utilising Graham Gibbs's Reflective Cycle. Subsequently, an evaluation of myself through the application of Johari window model to understand and enhance my self-disclosure, self-awareness together with self-discovery will be included. Afterword, identification and justification of my career aspiration together with creation of 5 years' personal development plan will be also included to mention all the important stages in detail.

2. Refection of previous learning

Reflection is the strategy to realise and enhance practice that we achieve from previous experience and this is a way to process our feelings and thought about an incident and create an opportunity for us to approach a terminology with our feelings and thoughts regarding it (Reynolds, 1998). Key points of reflection are following:

❖ This is an evaluation, exploration, analysis and explanation of an instance rather than simply just a description

❖ This often implies exposing errors, anxieties, weakness together with success and strengths

❖ It is essential to extract most essential parts on the instance on which reflection work will be carried out rather than select the whole story which may result of describing instead of reflecting.

2.1 What is implied in reflection?

This is an important part of thinking and learning where reflective learning signifies the purpose to learn from previous or current experience (Moon, 2004). This is the process of thinking in order to obtain understanding and develop new learning. According to (Gholami and Biria, 2014) flowing are the significant prospects of a reflection activity

❖ **Create intuition of experience:** People often don't learn from experience by itself where with reflection an analysis can be carried out to make a clear meaning indeed that would lead to learning.

❖ **Repetition:** reflection implies checking an incident or event for many times to identify the outcomes from several viewpoints.

❖ **Integrity**: Reflection is significantly connected with honesty and integrity. This should be fair and honest representation of an event.

❖ **Clarity:** Greater clarity can be brought with a reflection activity which would assist at all steps of planning, performing, and effectively reviewing actions.

❖ **Understanding:** reflection assist to understand and get deeper insight of an activity instead of just thought.

I have employed Graham Gibbs's Reflective Cycle developed in 1988 to reflect on my prior learning which is significant to assist an individual to learn from past experience. This model involves six stages to understand and learn to bring positivity and enhancement in personal life and career path.

Graham Gibbs's Reflective Cycle developed in 1988 [1]

Description

This reflective statement is mainly based on my previous learning during staying in UK where I have entered in UK in June 2009 to study BA (Hons) in Applied Accounting at Anglia Ruskin University and have graduated in 2012 with first class. After my graduation I have finished my MSc in Accounting & Finance from BPP University with Merit and then I have enrolled for Doctor of Business Administration at UWS. Over the last few years I have had different experiences where some of them was positive and some of them was negative where I have faced so many difficulties and challenges to finish my studies. However, those difficulties have

---

[1] Gibbs, G.R., 2015. *Learning and qualitative data analysis with information technology: the role of exploration* (Doctoral dissertation, University of Huddersfield).

prepared me to face the challenges in life and inspired me for better future which is the most motivational factor for studying at DBA program.

Feelings

I have both positive and negative feelings about my previous learning where I have positive feelings because undertaken programs (both BA & MSc) in both universities (Anglia Ruskin, BPP) were very well designed to enhance my skills and expertise where I have developed my knowledge about accounting, Audit, Tax, Business analysis, performance management, leadership, financial management and corporate governance significantly where most of the topics have been delivered during class lecture and tutorial spontaneously and clearly.

Behaviour of teachers has also created very positive feelings where I have experienced that all the teachers are very eager to assist students to develop their knowledge and understanding which was unseen in my back home. Any problem I faced whether it is academic or personal I got help from my teachers. Nevertheless, I have some negative feelings as well, especially regarding administration of university where I faced very unhealthy environment to get any support. It was very challenging even to talk with them where they were pretending, they are owner of me, and I have no right to talk with them. Moreover, sometimes both universities demonstrated that they only care about money not about student where once I could not pay my tuition fees, university did not allow me to attend the class.

Evaluation

Previous learning in UK has produced many positive benefits into my academic and personal life where I have developed so many skills and expertise to face the future challenges. Moreover, during my previous study I have been given the opportunity to perform activities with the people from diverse backgrounds where this diversity gave me a scope to learn about different culture, enhanced my innovation skills and developed my problem-solving skills and experts.

Furthermore, activities like class presentation and group work have developed my public speaking skills significantly where it was a matter of fear to communicate with other people. Nevertheless, I have experienced that some teachers were not caring about the student and did not give the opportunity to ask question which created confusion into me about the topics, but group work assisted a lot to overcome these kinds of challenges.

Analysis

My experience regarding my previous is mainly positive because of environment of universities where each of the university has their own library to study and sufficient online resources which is easily accessible to research and gather knowledge and this type of facilities even weren't in my dream. The opportunity to work within the group has also provided me positive experiences where most of the group members wear motivated and happy to help and this group work has provided me deep insight regarding my culture.

I was very afraid to speak public this is mainly because of lack of practices and weakness in English language as it is not my first language. However, Public speaking is a great self-esteem booster, significant to share views with other and assistance to enhance critical thinking (Behnke and Sawyer, 1999). However, various group activities and class presentation have provided me opportunities to overcome this problem significantly. Moreover, most of the lecturers I had during my previous learning wear very experienced and delivered lectures very effective way and they involved students in many practicing activities which also created positive experience for me.

However, study timetables weren't much organised where so many classes cancelled even without any notice and didn't have any recovery classes and that's why I suffered a lot during exam time. Moreover, sometimes administration of the universities was reluctant to listen to our opinion even in the time we are right, and this created negative experience for me.

Conclusion

The experience regarding my previous learning is significantly positive even I had some difficulties and challenges regarding behaviour of administration people, timetables and financial difficulties. My prior learning has created an impression that effective teamwork with accountability and responsibility is very essential to be successful instead of working along. Furthermore, it also developed my public presentation skill significantly through different activities and group work.

Moreover, my pervious learnings have also created an impression that negative feedback is very essential to correct the mistakes and make me perfect. I strongly consider that skill, expertise and knowledge I have attained from my prior learning will support me to be effective in personal life and professional life.

Action Plan

In future, I will develop positive relationship with people from the first day of activity as group work is very essential to be successful and I will prepare myself to face any situation whether it is positive or negative. I would invest more time to overcome the problem of public speaking to express my opinion to other people and try to build positive relationship with administration people.

3. Current position

At present I am studying Doctorate of Business Administration (DBA) program which has been started in April 2016 which has two phases where phase one consists of four compulsory modules including Strategic Thinking &Value Management (STVM), Strategy into Action (SIA), Leadership for professional development, Research Methodology where each of them requires individual assignment consists of company report, evidence review and reflection on leadership development. Phase two consists of researching a management problem through action learning sets to complete a 60,000 words thesis over the last two years.

I have completed first two subjects of phase one (SIA, STVM) and close to finish final two subjects (Leadership for professional development, Research Methodology) after that I will move to my final destination to 60,000 words thesis.

Since I have started DBA program, I have gained some inevitable skill to be successful in the business for instance, identification problems those are being facing by the organisations, how to solve those problem, how to add valve to the organisation and how to implement successful strategies within the organisation. Moreover, throughout the DBA program I am having opportunity to work with people from different background in the Action learning sets which has created an impression into me that teamwork is behind the success of anything.

Before I have started DBA, I have completed MSc in Accounting & Finance from BPP University and BA (Hons) in Applied Accounting from Anglia Ruskin University which has allowed me to gain vast knowledge on Accounting and finance related issue. Moreover, I am an affiliate member of Association of Chartered Certified Accountants (ACCA), i.e. passed all the papers but no practical experience yet which also has assisted me to achieve knowledge in accounting and finance related topics. Nevertheless, I have lack of experience and expertise in management related topics which was one of the key factors that motivated me to study on

DBA program because this program is mainly focused on management related issues and provides deeper insights on this topic.

As I have career aspiration to work at the executive level of the company where management skills and self-awareness are vital requirement therefore, I found this useful to identify my strengths & weaknesses, explore the opportunities and eliminate and reduce threat where SWOT analysis is very useful tool.

3.1 Self- awareness

Self-awareness is the process of having a diaphanous understanding of an individual's personality including strengths, weaknesses, beliefs, thoughts, emotions and motivation that allows an individual to understand other people and, how they perceive about that individual (Silvia and Phillips, 2013). Nevertheless, Asendorpf et al. (1996) defined self-awareness as understanding and recognizing how an individual's emotions affect own interactions of an individual with others and effect on emotional state of other people which involves being aware about own emotional state.

Therefore, prior to the reflection on past learning experience, I have found useful to utilise SWOT analysis as a self-awareness tool because it will assist to maximise strengths and diminish weaknesses of an individual. Moreover, it can assist an individual to understand preference and personality traits.

3.2 Strengths (Internal and positive)

This is internal positive aspects of an individual that are under your control, for instance things where an individual really good at and value that an individual has to offer, etc.

Academic results: I have achieved great academic results during my previous studies which is one of my great strengths where I have completed my BA(Hons) in Applied Accounting with first class (74% mark on average) and completed my MSc in Accounting & Finance with merit (63%).

Moreover, I am affiliate member of Association of Chartered Certified Accountants (completed 14 papers out of 14) which is the leading professional body for chartered accountant. In addition, I have successfully completed first two subject (SIA, STVM) of DBA program with more than 60% marks which is a great achievement in my academic life and this academic result will differentiate me from other which can be great advantage for my career.

Work Experience: I have been working as a Payroll coordinator at Selfridges for last four years which has been giving me practical experience and deeper insights regarding management role and this practical experience might be one of the sources of competitive advantages in future.

Time management: I am committed to maintain accurate time management in my academic and working places where till now I have completed my all the assignments and work responsibilities in a timely manner and always meet the deadline set for work.

Team worker: I am very good team worker where I am very happy to assist team member with my knowledge and expertise to achieve desired goal. My positive team working often help to build relationship with people where I strongly believe building relationship rather than complaining about another member is more significant to be successful.

Technology: I am able to adopt to any technology and changes in technology where I have efficient knowledge on modern technological devices and can operate effectively.

3.3 Weakness (Internal and negative)

These are internal negative aspects of an individual that are under control of an individual and which can be improved by action and practices. For instance, limited knowledge, lack of experience.

Lack of management knowledge: All of my educational background is on accounting and finance related but have not got any management insights during my previous study. However, management knowledge is essential to achieve career objective and goals which is one of my significant weakness.

Patience is not virtue: I always feel in rush to complete any task and I have lack of patience in regarding anything where I often get annoyed with the people who are slow moving during the completion of given tasks. This weakness sometimes creates obstacle during team work as other people feel annoyed with me as well for my lack of patience.

Lack of professional experience: I have already completed all of my academic parts of chartered accounting but still I am not full member of ACCA because of lack of professional experience which requires 3 years' professional experience to claim full membership.

3.4 Opportunities (External and positive)

Positive external conditions of an individual which are not within control of that individual but if these can be explored will be advantageous factor for that individual.

DBA Program: This program is mainly focused on management knowledge and leadership expertise where I have lack of management knowledge. Therefore, this program might assist me to learn about management knowledge & expertise and assist me to fill the gaps in this area.

Enhance communication skill: I have been doing lots of presentation during lecture and tutorial time in the DBA program which is assisting me to develop my public spiking skill and this skill would be source of competitive advantage in career path.

CMI qualification: I am already affiliate member of ACCA, and I will be qualified member of Chartered Management Institute with the DBA qualification which will differentiate me from the other candidates during job interview.

3.5 Threat (external and negative)

Negative external conditions which are not within the control of an individual but the effect of which an individual might be able to minimise.

New regulation: As an international student I must comply the regulations imposed by regulatory authority and governments where any adverse change may hamper my study and personal way of thinking. Any non-compliance might be the result of deportation from the country.

Tuition fees: I have to provide substantial amount of tuition fees to continue my study and I will not able to pay required fess I will be unable to finish my DBA program. As international Student I am restricted to work 20 hours per week which is not even enough for my transport and accommodation cost and my father has to pay all of my tuition's fees and therefore any adverse changes my father's income may negatively affect my study.

A synopsis of my personal SWOT analysis can be found in the following diagram.

Summary SWOT Analysis

Strengths	Weaknesses
1. Great Academic Results in previous study 2. Long time work experiance 3. Effecient in time management 4. Good team worker 5. Effecient with modern technology.	1. Lack of knowledge in management related topics. 2. Lack of patence in task completion 3. Lack of professional experiance
Opportunities	Threats
1. DBA Program 2. Enhance communication skill 3. CMI qualification	1. Comply with changing rules and regulations. 2. Providing substantial amount of tuition fees 3. fluctuation in UK economy

Personal SWOT analysis

Source: Authors own creation.

4. Continuous professional development (CPD)

CPD is the method by which professionals develop and sustain their knowledge, skills and expertise (Collin, Van der Heijden and Lewis, 2012). The movement of the world is ever faster and therefore constant CPD is vital to assist current role and responsibilities along with facilitating career progression and this is all about enhancing capabilities, skills, knowledge and expertise to remain compliant and effective (Megginson and Whitaker, 2007).

4.1 Main landscapes of the CPD process

❖ This should be a recorded process.

❖ This is self-directed for instance, driven by individual but not by employer.

❖ Emphasis on reflective learning, review and learning from experience.

❖ Assist an individual to establish development goals and objectives

❖ This engage both informal & formal learning.

Since I have started DBA at UWS, I have got deeper insight regarding business strategy, how to add value to the organisation, how to bring change within the organisation, leadership & professional development which are essential for continuous professional development.

Modules in first trimester (SIA, STVM) empowered me to carry detailed analysis of the problem, make recommendations to solve the problem and outline the strategy to bring the changes within the organisation which might assist me to achieve my career goal & objective. Since I have started DBA, I got deep insight on the following areas.

Business strategy:

Strategy is the direction and scope of an organisation to attain advantages over the competitors over the long-term through its configuration of resources and competences to meet the markets demand and to accomplish expectations of stakeholder (Johnson, Scholes and Whittington, 2008). From STVM & SIA Modules I have got understanding how to plan organisational strategy and how to implement strategy within an organisation to meet the demands of shareholders and other stakeholders. I have got better understanding on the following three level of business strategies.

Three Levels of Strategy

- *Corporate level:* board of directors, CEO & administration [Highest]

- *Business level:* business and corporate managers [Middle]

- *Functional level:* Product, geographic, and functional area managers [Lowest]

Three levels of strategy[2]

---

[2] Johnson, G., Scholes, K. and Whittington, R., (2008). *Exploring corporate strategy: text & cases.* Pearson education.

Leadership

Leadership is a significant activity of management which assist to enhance efficiency and to achieve goals & objective of the organisation and effective leadership is significant to initiate action, motivate employees, providing guidance, create confidence build moral and work environment (Smythe and Norton, 2007). From SIA, leadership and professional module I have gained an understanding regarding the significance of leadership to solve the problem and achieve desired goal of the organisation.

Change management

Today's financial and business world is even more volatile and each and every day they are facing threat to is existence and therefore, for its sustainability each and every entity needs to go through change process (Hughes, 2007). From SIA module I have gained detail understanding how change process works and how to implement change and how to manage resistance to the change within an organisation and personal life.

Public speaking

Many people are worried to engage in public speaking, but it is the most significant form of communication to express own opinion and without this communication skills, the capability to develop in life and in working life might be nearly unmanageable (Behnke and Sawyer, 1999). Although I was very afraid to speak publicly, and it is largely because of lack of opportunity to talk publicly but I have been getting opportunity during the DBA program as I have been engaging many formative and summative presentation. Now I feel more confident to talk publicly then earlier starting DBA and I believe that over the next few years with DBA program with UWS my public speaking will be fluent and smooth.

Diversity

According to The American Council on Education (ACE) Diversity enriches the educational experience, promotes personal growth, strengthens the workplace and communities, enhances economic competitiveness (Anon, 2016). During the DBA program I am having opportunity to study and perform group work with people from different background and as a result of this I got understanding regarding various culture and different way of doing things which is assisting me to become more efficient & effective.

Critical thinking

Critical thinking is the evaluation and objective analysis of an issue due to form a judgement (Knowles, 1999). Since I have started DBA program all the tutors have been inspiring me be a critical thinker to form any decision and judgement whether it is in academic or in personal life and as a result of this, I have been following the following matters before making any judgement.

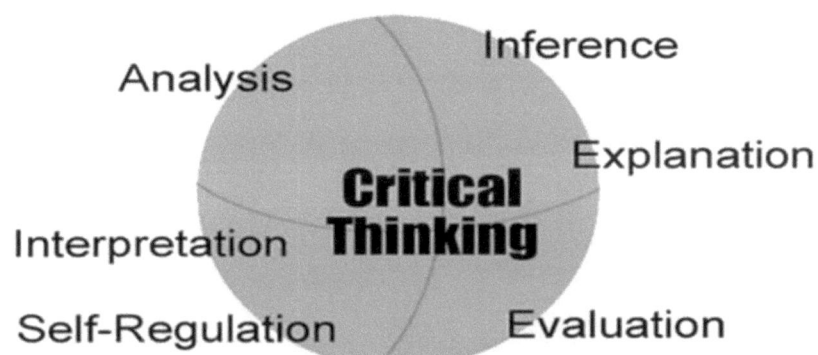

Core critical thinking skills[3]

4.3 Evaluation of personal development:

For evaluation of my personal development I would like to utilise Johari window developed by Harrington Ingham & Joseph Luft in 1955 which is a significant tool for demonstrating and enhancing self-awareness, and reciprocated understanding among different characters within a group (Biech, 2008). Four regions of Johari window are following:

---

[3] Flores, K.L., Matkin, G.S., Burbach, M.E., Quinn, C.E. and Harding, H., (2012). Deficient critical thinking skills among college graduates: Implications for leadership. *Educational Philosophy and Theory*, *44*(2), pp.212-230.

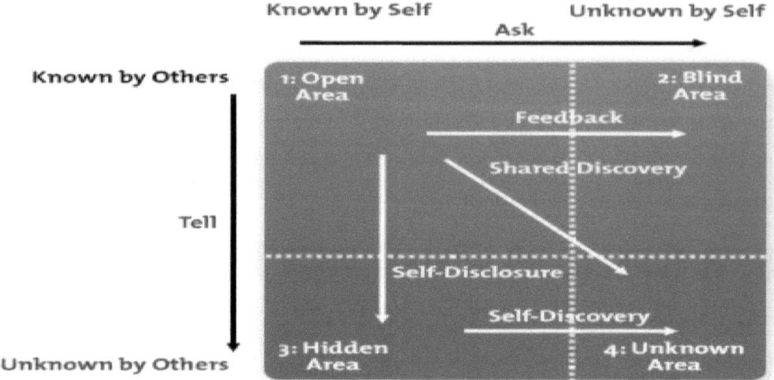

This framework involves following adjectives to provide a potential description of an individual.

Johari adjectives A Johari Window consists of 55 adjectives used to describe the participant, in alphabetical order:

- able
- accepting
- adaptable
- bold
- brave
- calm
- caring
- cheerful
- clever
- complex
- confident

- dependable
- dignified
- energetic
- extroverted
- friendly
- giving
- happy
- helpful
- idealistic
- independent
- ingenious

- intelligent
- introverted
- kind
- knowledgeable
- logical
- loving
- mature
- modest
- nervous
- observant
- organized

- patient
- powerful
- proud
- quiet
- reflective
- relaxed
- religious
- responsive
- searching
- self-assertive
- self-conscious

- sensible
- sentimental
- shy
- silly
- spontaneous
- sympathetic
- tense
- trustworthy
- warm
- wise
- witty

Paradigm of Johari window human capital[4]

I have utilised Johari window to evaluate my relationship with other students of the DBA program when I have started DBA program with UWS. At the beginning program at April 2016 I wasn't much aware about other students and they weren't aware about me either and therefore, very few numbers of matters were in the open area & blind spot where unknown and hidden areas were much bigger than compare to other two.

---

[4] Shenton, A.K., (2007). Viewing information needs through a Johari Window. *Reference Services Review*.

However, I knew very well that this massive unknown and hidden area will be a big obstacle to my success and therefore, I have started interacting with them and building positive relationship during class lecture, tutorial group work and outside of study time, for instance watching movies, participate in different games and traveling into different locations and all of this activities have been assisting me to minimise unknown and hidden areas and enlarge my open area. With the assistance of people from DBA program and workplace I have developed following Johari window.

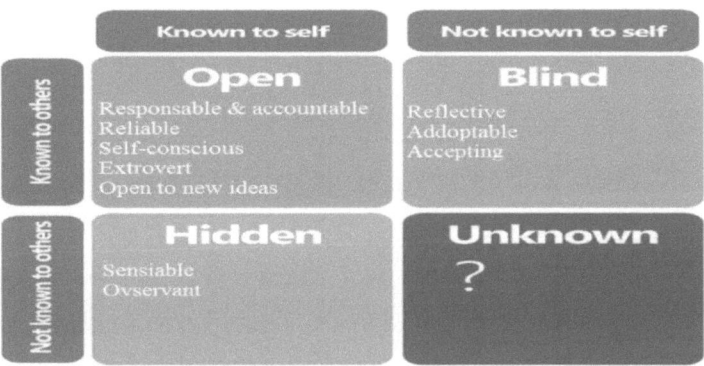

My personal Johari windows

Source: Author's own creation

5. Future professional & personal development (over the next 5 years)

Career expectation or ambition are simply the goals and objectives of an individual to achieve in either current profession or in desired profession in future which clearly outlines what an individual need or wants from his/her profession (Boys and Kirkland, 1988).

5.1 Personal development plan for next 5 years

Goals	Class of development	What will I need to achieve?	Development provider	How I will measure success	Duration & potential cost	Deadline
Complete first phase of DBA program.	Academic	Complete research methodology & Leadership modules	Class lectures & tutorial group University Library Study on own time at home.	Get research proposal accepted. Complete both Leadership & Research modules successfully.	3 months	19/11/2016
Start working for a ACCA listed Accounting firm	Professional	Create a great CV and apply for job.	ACCA listed Firms Different job sites	Get a job as a practice accountant.	8 months	31/05/216
Enhance public speaking and presentation skill	Professional/ academic/ personal	Start talking with other people regarding anything important.	Attend training class provided by external PDP institute.	Able to express my own thoughts & ideas clearly and fluently to others	12 months £200-£250 per class	30/09/2017
Acquire basic & advance knowledge of Sage accounting	Professional/ personal	Enrol for a course to learn Sage program.	http://www.sage.co.uk/	Can use Sage software and services effectively &efficiently	18 months	31/03/2018

18

Achieve full ACCA membership	Professional/ Personal	Get work experience from ACCA listed firm.	ACCA Listed Audit & accounting firm.	Approve by ACCA as full member.	24 months	30/09/2018
Complete DBA program	Academic/ personal	Complete the main research face on time and at an academic good standard	London campus of University of the west of Scotland.	Gain approval from DBA committee.	30 months	31/03/2019
Graduate teaching assistant of any UK University.	Professional/ Personal	Complete the DBA program. Prepare a great CV and apply for job.	Any UK college & university	Get a job as a Graduate teaching assistant	36 months	30/09/2019
To be a lecturer of a well-known University	Professional/ Personal	Complete the DBA program. Get experienced as a graduate teaching assistant.	Different well-known universities all over the world	Get a job as a university Lecturer.	5 years	30/09/2021.

19

5.2 Personal objectives

Short time Goal (Next 12 months)
Over the next 12 months I would like to complete first phase of DBA program with the help of class lectures & tutorial and start working for an ACCA listed accounting firm which is a professional development and attend training class provided by external PDP institute to enhance public speaking and presentation skill.

Medium term Goal (Next 2- 3 years)
By the next two to three years I would like to learn SAGE accounting and get full ACCA membership for my personal & professional development. Moreover, I would like to get approval of my research from UWS DBA committee.

Long term Goal (Beyond 3 years)
My long-term goal primarily focus on my professional achievement where I would like to be a graduate teaching assistant of any UK University and finally become a lecturer of a well-known University anywhere in the world which will lead to my final destiny.

6. Conclusion

Personal development plan (PDP) is very useful tool to assist the enhancement of an independent learning approach, support career development, create a mechanism to enhance employability skills and imparts a way to record professional and personal development and to record the outcomes of learning (Eisele et al., 2013). Formation of this PDP has assisted me to analyse my past and present learning & development and create a plan to develop my academic, personal & professional skills overall to achieve my future goals & objectives.

In this PDP I have reflected on my prior learning from previous universities and analysed my current position by utilising SWOT analysis which identified some threats & weaknesses which need to be addressed to achieve my goals & objectives.

Knowledge & skills I have learnt form DBA program for instance business strategy, change management, leadership, public speaking & diversity will be great asset to achieve my goals. Overall, this PDB has created an opportunity to identify the skills & expertise I already adhere to and the gaps and weakness to be corrected to a lecturer of a university.

Reference

Anon, (2012). *On the Importance of Diversity in Higher Education.* [online] Available at: http://www.acenet.edu/news-room/Documents/BoardDiversityStatement-June2012.pdf [Accessed 19 Sep. 2016].

Behnke, R. and Sawyer, C. (1999). Public speaking procrastination as a correlate of public speaking communication apprehension and self-perceived public speaking competence. Communication Research Reports, 16(1), pp.40-47.

Biech, E. (2008). The Pfeiffer book of successful team-building tools. San Francisco, CA: Pfeiffer.

Boys, C. and Kirkland, J. (1988). Degrees of success. London: Kingsley.

Collin, K., Van der Heijden, B. and Lewis, P. (2012). Continuing professional development. International Journal of Training and Development, 16(3), pp.155-163.

Ellwood, F. (2011). Understanding the importance of a personal development plan. *Dental Nursing*, 7(3), pp.160-163.

Eisele, L., Grohnert, T., Beausaert, S. and Segers, M. (2013). Employee motivation for personal development plan effectiveness. Euro J of Training and Dev, 37(6), pp.527-543.

Gholami, H. and Biria, R. (2014). Reflective journal writing and learner autonomy. JLL, 5(3), pp.138-142.

Gibbs, G. (1988). Learning by doing. [London]: FEU.

Hughes, M. (2007). The Tools and Techniques of Change Management. Journal of Change Management, 7(1), pp.37-49.

Johnson, G., Scholes, K. and Whittington, R. (2008). Exploring corporate strategy. Harlow: Prentice Hall.

Kotter, J. (1995). The New Rules: How to Succeed in Today's Post-Corporate World. Free Press.

Knowles, E. (1999). The Oxford dictionary of quotations. Oxford: Oxford University Press.

Moon, J. (2004). A handbook of reflective and experiential learning. London: RoutledgeFalmer.

Megginson, D. and Whitaker, V. (2007). Continuing professional development. London: Chartered Institute of Personnel and Development.

Rouse, K. (2005). *Personal development*. South Melbourne: Oxford University Press.

Reynolds, M. (1998). Reflection and Critical Reflection in Management Learning. Management Learning, 29(2), pp.183-200.

Silvia, P. and Phillips, A. (2013). Self-awareness Without Awareness? Implicit Self-focused Attention and Behavioral Self-regulation. Self and Identity, 12(2), pp.114-127.

Smythe, E. and Norton, A. (2007). Thinking as Leadership/Leadership as Thinking. Leadership, 3(1), pp.65-90.